For Hank + Linda —

So you know what
The crazy neighbor is up to —

With my best wishes for
your thriving in beauty — and
in blessing —

Steven

THE WINGS OF WHAT YOU SAY

THE WINGS OF
WHAT YOU SAY

∾

99 Sonnets by
STEVEN NIGHTINGALE

RAINSHADOW EDITIONS
THE BLACK ROCK PRESS
2013

Cloth Edition:
ISBN: 978-1-891033-63-6

Trade Paper Edition:
ISBN: 978-1-891033-64-3

Library of Congress Control Number: 2013947914

The Black Rock Press
University of Nevada, Reno Reno, NV 89557-0244
www.blackrockpress.org
Printed in the United States of America

Cover Image:
"Cranes and Setting Sun"
Japanese Woodblock Print. 1902

The Black Rock Press would like to thank the
Nell J. Redfield Foundation for their support of this book

For Bob and Sylvia Blake

—Who show us how to live with generosity, intelligence, and grace

Contents

Sonnets   1

Another Worker Without a Pension   2

Let's Be Plain and Ordinary Together   3

Crazy Even When Young   4

Benediction of Desire, and a Joke   5

That Question We Ask Ourselves   6

They Call It Stupid Clay   7

Failing, Thank Heaven, To See Yourself   8

She Admits To Have Changed a Little   9

Beauty Is   10

A History of Name-Calling   11

Brief Notes on Your Mind   12

Places   13

You Are Not Obligated to Die Miserably   14

How We Find It   15

In a Bar, the Andalusian Vase   16

Making a Note to Ourselves   17

The Prophet Next Door   18

Natural Selection Gets Funny   19

King's Canyon   20

Light on a Lake in the High Sierra   21

Another Day's Work   22

Just a Singing Girl with a Rock   23

Children without Sentiment   24

From the Santa Cruz Mountains   25

What You Say   26

If Words Are Good for Something, It's …   27

A Little Bit of Twilight Learning   28

Well, Would You?   29

The Man Who Wanted To Be Kept   30

Idolatry   31

Would You Be Mirror or Flame? 32

Some Days 33

He Questions Himself 34

We Surrender Mind, Then Everything 35

Our Leaders Explain Themselves 36

The Happy Album of Karl Hocker 37

Those Jazzy Smart Guys 38

Gimme That Old-Time Religion 39

Why Staring Is Thought To Be Discourteous 40

They've Got a Lot To Do 41

Messiah 42

How We Work with Him 43

War-Monger's Lament 44

The Hostess Apologizes 45

The Torturer Speaks 46

And So Handsome! 47

Rwanda Is Our Future 48

As the Oceans Rise 49

If I May Sum Up? Comment, Perhaps? 50

Lovely; and That Soul, for Heaven's Sake 51

After Work, Mountains, Wars, You Have 52

The News We Need 53

O Boccaccio! 54

Torcello 55

Cutting Open the Aloe 56

From the Ridge to the Beach at Tunitas Creek 57

Big Sur 58

Second Storm of the Redwood Forest 59

O That Thar Love 'n Soul Thang 60

Earth, A Question or Two 61

What Changed 62

O These Ordinary Women 63

Her Sweat 64

A Breeze in my Wife's Garden 65

Naked Season   66

The Open Country of her Loving   67

Prayer of One Parent One Day   68

At Four, Sleepwalking   69

Her Ballet Class in Granada, Age Four   70

For my Daughter   71

A Scrimmage with Death   72

Women in the Next Office   73

The High School English Teacher   74

Portrait of a Neighbor   75

She Is of the Community of Friends   76

A Gal   77

Are You Just Yourself?   78

A Modest Alternative to Enslavement   79

Reader, Just by Way of Explanation   80

Interview Questions   81

Our Momentary Infinite Work   82

She Seems To Be Changed   83

Shining One   84

Light, Salvation, the Rest of the Stuff   85

Somebody Has To. You.   86

Who Was That Guy, Anyway?   87

Reader, If I Might Mention One Small Thing   88

Replacing Yourself with the Original Model   89

Reader, Believe Me,   90

A House for You   91

Moving Right Along   92

Writing for You, Reader   93

Showing Us   94

Bemused Inevitable Unity of Things   95

Try This   96

Raw Materials   97

We Love Ordinary and Daily Language   98

After the Cataclysm of Suffering   99

Introduction

IN THE COURSE OF MANY READINGS of sonnets in the last years, certain questions, on occasion, have been directed to this bedraggled sonneteer, to wit: What on earth are you doing? Such radical declarations in verse, in so antique a form...isn't this rather sentimental? Aren't these subjects a bit fantastical? Impossible?

I think these inquiries entirely justified, since the practice of writing a sonnet a day is somewhat uncommon presently. It is a useful form, a pattern and an offering, capable of strange initiatives. One thinks of the DNA molecule, which might make a fingertip, a brain cell, a valve in the heart. One thinks of a circuit board, used to decode the light of distant stars, to investigate the genetics of families of flowering plants. Yet we know more about distant stars, flowering plants, and neural networks, than we do about other subjects common in our daily experience. Say, for instance, beauty. Or grace, the minutiae of our pleasures, the pressure of history, the precise exaltations of spirit; or even the passage of light through a glass of water.

Our experiments have overcome our experience. Our power has debased our understanding. Our politics hold in contempt our hopes for safety. And doctrine and habit confine our sense of the sacred.

The sonnet, like any art form, is at the beginning of its powers. For it can be used to answer an urgent calling: to know, beyond material progress, the beauty, grace, and understanding that can give form and meaning to such progress. This calling is ordinary, made daily, and made to all of us. If we answer, what happens then is what always happens: the mindful changes within that bring us to work in service of life, in honor of life, in thankfulness for life.

Without such a way forward, our progress will be our undoing, and our future will bring us so atrocious and unspeakable a degeneracy, that the catastrophes of the past centuries will look quaint.

These, I think, are the stakes. If this is sentiment, then poetry requires it. If this is overreaching, then I seek more companions, that our reach has yet more scope and mischief. If this is an impossible project, then we must thrive and laugh, and outfox impossibility together.

When it is inquired why I am hopeful, I say it is because I know that there is no force on earth so malevolent that it can resist you, reader, with a book in your hand. If these sonnets have a light within them, it is because you have illuminated them; they show just the light you give. I look around at the incomparable earth, and I know that what gives us a chance is the way its beauties have been entrusted to you.

I write because one day we will see before us an earth restored, lustrous, cherished. We will live in a community where justice comes first and generosity is common as paper. And after long labors, we will awaken to the promised hour when our children, hand in hand, in the morning light, walk forth onto the fields of their rejoicing.

—S. N.
King's Mountain, March 2013

Sonnets

Passage of earth, leading on to a season
Musical, lustrous; magic ship of reason

That bears us to our daft sure outpost
Of beauty, where tigers, stars, and children
Trade jokes and ideas; uncanny coast

Of a sea hidden within you, within all
Of us; the song that makes honey glow
In a secret hive in wilderness, to show
A way to workaday sweetness; lucent call

Of morning to the original soul—peaceful,
Mischievous, trustworthy—who will upend
A standard edition of world with needful

Bemused grace. Infinite reader, I am led
By a heaven in you, to make this seedbed.

Another Worker Without a Pension

It's just a job: to gather the trade winds
In a phrase, to mark a cadence that sends

Oceans onto the dance floor; to hold
And calm a volcano smoking in the garden
Near the peaches from paradise, whose gold

Grows alongside hot peppers and beans;
To tell the stories of sandstone, to sing
Of the day when you will move one wing,
Then another, how that day all you mean

Shows in the sky at morning; to speak
In the style of the crescent moon, pardon
Death his lurid hunger. With you, to seek

The centermost of peace, laughter at soul;
The turn of worlds in the running of a foal.

Let's Be Plain and Ordinary Together

It's true, there's a wildcat in the pantry,
Falcons in your hat. To live wide and free

In this homely destination of soul, means
That we are here, friends, together, talking
In the sunlight as twenty antelope careen

Around the table, as from the next room
We hear books cartwheeling off the shelves,
Novels opening, women standing, themselves
At last, transfigured at last—whatever doom

Or triumph they suffered in their story, now
They set aside, for a chance to be walking
Curiously through a meadow, as oaks bow

Before bullsnake, honeybee, and peacock,
Before paradise irrepressible in plain rock.

Crazy Even When Young

It's just that I never felt solid,
Fixed in flesh, groomed, known, glib,

Ready for battle. I lived a crossfire
Of events. Ripped, guttering, stormstruck—
Such was flesh. Each night on a high wire

I walked in raving inquisitorial winds. Just
Outside my door in the morning, I had
To wrangle wild horses stamping the dust
In the city light. Then to speak, I had

To hush the silver clanging of the moon,
The sea-waves' harp soft and sunstruck,
All the natural carnival of mind, monsoon

And chamber music of wit, the rock and roll
Of the heart, the pandemonium of the soul.

Benediction of Desire, and a Joke

What if the soul has desire? What if
You want radiance only; what if

Light comes with a homely calling—
First and future calling, one you always
Knew? You are visiting here. The falling

Into form, begins a wonder: to be
In the guest-house of flesh. You are liberty
And imprisonment, exultation and malady,
Theophany, smoke-puff, sorrow, integrity:

Yet rough savory light signals within
A wakefulness. What of you never decays
Has just this traveling—through the din,

Rancid distraction, lurid haze and word—
Coming home to a joke: heaven is learned.

That Question We Ask Ourselves

Look around you. Do you think you have
Air, light, earth, story and circumstance,

Songlines and the exultations of softness?
Well you do. And then what? You do,
Yet what if this world were one address

Of heaven? Our address. Word, proposition
And riddle, joke, testimony, and treasure,
High-jinks, hope, ideas, benediction:
All this, and beyond all faith. A feather

For wings you are making, is what
Every day will be—if you will undo
The darkness that is yourself, the strut

Of the swindling human. Look around you.
What if world was made to see through?

They Call It Stupid Clay

Calculating clay of the body, one day
You will see it is where the worlds say:

Metamorphosis. What is this change,
You will ask, into soil and stars, river
And moth, rain drop, mountain range—

What is this change? Yet it is no more
Wondrous than tides, revolution of earth
Around the sun, or at first light the perch
Of a meadowlark, who for heaven will pour

Song into the sapphire glass of hours.
Your heart is rhythm, not mere sliver
Of muscle; more music and wildflowers

Than brute tissue. Clay is revelation.
Flesh is terror, then joy: emancipation.

Failing, Thank Heaven, To See Yourself

Rambunctious sweetness of earth, yet still
It is first note and preface. The oracular trill

Of a hawk opens a door to another century,
Another overture, another domain of mind.
Coyotes visit concert halls, a snow flurry

Turns to sunlight. Death belongs to you,
Like a toy soldier. Go ahead, summon
A comet, take a ride and learn the reason
Poems are written with starlight for ink. You

Listen, you learn how to go skylarking
On trustworthy earth; the practical is divine,
Story beyond the famished dog barking

Who is history. All heavens are here.
Life is known only in a broken mirror.

She Admits To Have Changed a Little

To be nothing, is beginning again. You
Were constructed of sawdust and glue,

Until you struck a match, and learned
To give thanks when you were ashes.
What you were worth, you have spurned.

No one sees herself. What you want
Is stories rambling off in light to origin
And destination and work—not vicious rant
Of the news. Laughter will marry reason.

I watch you woven by light; your vision
Will reconstruct sight. When mountain passes
Are stanzas in stone, with earthly concision

Stand and speak them. Your emotion
Is idea; body is mind; breath, devotion.

Beauty Is

Winsome lover in the bed of world, she
Is sweat and hope. With her pleasure, she

Bends rivers and paints wing feathers, she
Calls shooting stars across the sky, she
Passes her hand over the afternoon sea

And in the pattern of whitecaps touched
By sunlight, we find the treasure map
The mind needs, if we would see brushed
Into place, a future of grace. A petty trap

In the present, she has blown apart with
Her dynamite of mischief, first wild free
Uncanny play every day in the world, kiss

And sensual voltage of soul—we are sure:
We belong to beauty. Earth belongs to her.

A History of Name-Calling

The light in you whirling: right then
By soft velocity of beauty, you ascend

Into the original world. They called it
Dizziness. A strange wind bore you off
Into the future, where you found the wit

To return to us, bemused with love, full
Of laughter and helpfulness. They called it
Disturbed functioning. In the garden, you sit
Among storm-fronts of flowers, and mull

And search, whisper, understand—until
Your words are all petals, you are lost
In the candor of the planet, and you fill

Your flesh with a first and final song.
They called it madness, all history long.

Brief Notes on Your Mind

Mind is stone and light, river, comet,
Trust and story, gut, sun, sonnet,

Stageset of centuries, ship whose sails
Catch trade winds of time, to search
For your work. Leave behind buried jails

Of everything you have been ever,
And ride the wild horse of the sun,
Hoof beats like heartbeats, joy undone
And made as you wander and suffer,

As you answer and you remember,
Working as bedraggled slave of earth,
Safe beyond the stars, you assemble

A life, a life, your miracle of grief
Not of world: in the world, at peace.

Places

They await: places with upwelling of beauty,
Raw insurrection, slow-dance and integrity

Beyond death. It may be a bend in a river,
Wild with eagles, soft sentence of willows;
Or a woman in a cafe, anonymous grace-giver—

She sits, reading a book, and all the earth
Will be seasoned by her understanding. It
May be two acrobats who together slip
The hard sinews of gravity, so to perch

On horns of the moon, rock all heaven,
Tumble into invisibility. It may be billows
Of sea-fog at strange liberty, that leaven

Long meadows with mystic shining report.
It may be you, heaven's secret consort.

You Are Not Obligated to Die Miserably

It can't be said too often—the world
You see, it's not there. You have furled

Opalescent story and possibility, fastened
It down, closed it within. But the winds,
Particolored and irresistible, veer and wend

Through this life and the next, they catch
And tease our tiny and comfortable order.
You'll have a wisping of stars at hand, whirr
And roar of rain forest at night in the match

You use to light a candle on the table where
You dine with the one you love. These winds
Are the weather of the mind, soul's care

For you every second, each hour, this day—
A thunder and the promise in what you say.

How We Find It

The climate of the heart, the atmosphere
Of the mind, bring life-storms: the mirror

Shatters, to honor your hope: to never
Defraud yourself again. In the place
Of a stamped image, in place of a clever

Knotted hide, crust, mask of world,
Suddenly from nothing you can compose
Yourself. You can be a cloud, a rose,
Summer, a child's toy; misshapen pearl

In an attic that one day, found by a child,
Begins to shine, because it gives the grace
Of prophecy. With you, the sacred: wild

And peaceable, forthright and secret, open
And invisible. Silent revelation. First reason.

In a Bar, the Andalusian Vase

Ordinary bar, coffee strong as cognac.
Necessary as sunlight, stronger than fact.

The room revolved around a blue-and-cream
Andalusian vase, left here by a grandfather
Of the grandfather who had it of the queen,

Disguised as a beggar. She sold it to him
For a loaf of bread, then vanished, in a gust
Of twilight. These shining ones, they trust
What is best in us, they want us to live

And live, they leave signposts and clues,
Stars and news; leave beauty so pure
That a vase in a bar glows and proves

That magnets of reality are everywhere—
A bar, a street, flower, any patch of air.

Making a Note to Ourselves

Let's explain it this way: space
Makes love with language. Every place

Will have its wild phrase, couplet, rhyme,
Craggy syllable, winged sentence, word
Within the nectary of beauties we find

When sound and meaning marry. Every place
Lives then, comes to mystery, wherever we
Are. Note, for example, a memorable taste
Of the tropics in a woman's musk, her liberty

And theology of pleasures, even as, outside,
It is snowing. Note, as you thrive, a tropicbird
Soaring along the coastline when you defied

All despair. Note the waterfall in your room,
The friend who teaches you to ride a typhoon.

The Prophet Next Door

To have them listen, it's helpful
To ride a chariot of fire, or to spell

A timely name of god late at night
With newborn stars, or to sing so that
Cohorts of lightning come into sight.

Yet a customary miracle is not less
Miracle. Even light in passage through
A glass of water. Can world come true
In one seed of a pomegranate, pressed

To find a sweetness far inside summer,
Like blood with seasoning of soul? Can that
Chariot be ordinary morning, its fire a burn

Of your own light? Are you an average man?
Or a plain woman, planets in your hand—

Natural Selection Gets Funny

Scarlet macaws: every morning repainted
Because light is an artisan who waited

Worlds ago to make this chance: a bird
Whose cries mocked heaven into laughter
At itself. It is the laughter that cured

The sickness of anyone you loved, anyone
You will love, forever. The macaws talk
About the time they had lightning among
Them, and passed a bolt around. They broke

That power in their beaks, in celebration:
Now storms love them. In their patter
Are tropical sonnets, impasto education.

Light is an artisan, looking for work.
The macaw: what light does with dirt.

King's Canyon

Where granite ridges stand high—sails
To catch the wind of universal gales,

So that this earth may turn; where
Wildflowers are tempest and delectation,
Soft minute heavenly testimony; where

Lakes watch the clouds, sun, stars,
Moon—then, brushed by the wind,
Show a light within; where the tars,
Quicksand, mistake, shame, chagrin,

Hatred and death-cult in our history
Are set aside forever, all degradation
Is undone, we see our plain story:

Soul is made of water, rock, and sky.
Like them we live, like them we die.

Light on a Lake in the High Sierra

By wind, water shows light. By mind,
World shows life. In this study we find

Movement of understanding on the surface
Of days that show a pattern of the divine
Always present, like the sun; then we cross

To another world within this one, which
Makes and remakes millennium and hours,
World final, phosphorescent in its powers,
By whose grace we may learn; and switch

Flesh for wild permanence, as we live
Here, now, together. These lakes shine
When music is made of a pulse we give

As we share all mind, give away
Everything all night, and every day.

Another Day's Work

It is you and the trade winds, together,
Who decide about the future. Weather

Of soul needs collaboration with air:
Gust, breeze, squall, blizzard, cyclone—
You and sky go rambling: fanfare

And steel clouds, azure flourishes, stone-
Shattering bolts of light, tropical heat
Like gold oil brushed on hours who shown
In sensual peace. Now, you complete

Yourself. As you give, so you must
Be this composer of mind-stuff, alone
And in company with world. Use the dust

You are. Wink and music, rain and light—
Someone must compose day and night.

Just a Singing Girl with a Rock

A little girl throws a flat stone on water,
In merriment it skips, then at her whisper

Turns to a blue heron, banks in beauty,
Rises in the summer air, moves high
Atop a spiral of heat, in mantic liberty

Leaves earth: then, combustion, blazing—
A comet crosses the sky to disappear
Into darkness perfected that runs clear
To heaven; and there it has its glazing

Of life, and flies to an appointed sun
To take its place as a planet, and try
To remember how one morning in fun

A girl skipped a stone across a pond,
And made life as she whispered a song.

Children without Sentiment

A child eating a tangerine sits on a wall
Of stones woven with flowers, bright shawl

Of sunlight and sea-mist about her beauty,
Which is antidote and deliverance. You
Learn from her: no horror, nor rank contumely

Of the human world today will touch her.
Rambunctious with blessing, she is sent here
To offer a coloratura of light, her clear
Studious planetary form; and with acid fear

We know that this world is fallen
Only because of us. What is true
Is what they will do: gather the pollen

Of the future and make honey. A white crow
In a child's hand is what we come to know.

From the Santa Cruz Mountains

Along the ridge, a meadow knits soft notes
Through the music of morning, in throats

Of quail and raven and red-tailed hawk,
Sonorous perfection of redwoods, in concord
With lush song and long phrasing of oak,

Slow crimson dance of madrone, as in
A ravine a cougar brings home the beauty
Of his hunt—the lame deer had a duty
To be feline. Beyond the meadows, a fin

Of a white shark in the old combustible peace
Of the ocean, as a humpback surges, a sword
Shattering the topaz, an ocean whose reach

Is all the way to light. The way to you.
Here is what you are. What we do.

What You Say

It's that what happens, happens inside
You. The span of the mind is as wide

As the earth, so that when waves fall
In their lapis confabulation, when they
Spread heaven over the shore, they call

In your voice. The holy red-tailed hawk
Lands atop a redwood that grows inside
A space in your body. When you cried
Out, it was known to eagles and the rock

Of wild mountains, it was known to stars
So distant, they are neighbors. The play
Of coyotes in a desert, music in country bars,

You find in your own phrase, this very day—
An eyelash, a solar flare, in what you say.

If Words Are Good for Something, It's...

Because in what you say is spring water
That bears melody, your clarity, to cure

The rancor of history. Because savory rhyme
Will taste of the earth, will taste like a wine
Just made that gives you liberty of mind

To be sidekick of uncanny ocean currents,
Companion to trade winds, legendary friend
To the raven, who in his ebony assurance
Will sass the gods, spread wings and bend

The light to show a glossiness within logic—
A close reasoning, a proposition, the design
And proof of beauty. Each word is a magic

Box. Open it up with the key of meaning.
You make the earth with such dreaming.

A Little Bit of Twilight Learning

Your notes, sounded at last the afternoon
Heaven sent them to you, when the loon

Cried out and on water the canter of light
Moved in concord with the beautiful grasses,
So that we traveled together inside twilight—

Your notes are needed just now, because
We can see how a cross-current of destiny
Runs in this meadow by the sea, university
Where you went to learn the secret laws

Of pastel rains and full iridescent rhythm
Of hummingbird's wings; honey-slow crashes
Of one continent into another, touch, jism,

Spice, hope, all there, our world's fair:
Common healing music, in your care.

Well, Would You?

To be transparent at will: can you trust
This new vanishing, in favor of the musk

Of a woman who reaches through to stars
In you? She knows how mischievous sky
Is married to earth, how country bars,

Barbarous canyons, hot peppers, coyotes,
Chrysanthemums and metaphysics, in a tryst
With life, bemused with verse, are seeds—
So many capsules of mind. Even the abyss

Is your rambunctious school. Would you
Learn from her how to love, to fly
With lustrous earth; learn homely, true,

Riptide storytelling of day and night—
Where what you see, is phrased by light?

The Man Who Wanted To Be Kept

I wondered, what was it in my hands
That you dismissed them? Fragrant lands,

A peach and a music, hope; springtime
Adventurous, suave, a spiced abundance;
All cadence of devotion and the rhyme

Of starlight with our every hour—I had
This prayer, that my hands for you
Would hold all this. If I could have had
A planet in my palm, that healing blue—

High cobalt, dialect of clouds—I would
Have given it to you, on the chance
That you would look, at last you would

See how we might love again. The way,
If you held me, I could never go away.

Idolatry

For millennia, on every continent; in space,
On every planet in every galaxy, in the taste

Of bread, music of stars in the desert,
Potent new moon, everywhere, always,
One warning: we are not fit to be dirt

If we honor image: the literal, given,
Exposed larval glittering. When we do,
It is gambol of desecration; heaven
Will not stop even to be ashamed. You

And I will not be worth shame. Love,
I learned hell does not exist. Highways
Of folly lead not to demons who shove

Us into a furnace. They lead to nothing—
Bakery of minds with idolatrous stuffing.

Would You Be Mirror or Flame?

The soul has sweet liquid that might
Be heated by the energy of your sight

In love. Your wilderness of gifts will
Concentrate that sweetness, so to make
The elixir. Then concentration, full

Fine tempering: in you, a polished mirror
Reflecting a light that leads you home.
Unless you fail. The elixir sweet and clear
May be lost, and leave brain and bone

Ridiculous in triumphs, soul-sweet liquid
Rancid with ignorance, roiling with a hate
Hidden in your courtesy, in a rapturous bid

To see your labor honored, your name backlit
By flames: infernal shining of your own wit.

Some Days

Some days, bitterness in my veins is riot
And burgeoning. I am cast down, in the quiet

Of a clean building, all a gaudy shambles
Of sorrow. Will the world never learn
That mercy is courage? That rambles

Of girls in blackberry shadow in the woods
Turn to comedy, delectation, learning, justice—
And justice is in bed with beauty? The goods
We covet boil, our demonic baubles, a grist,

Waste, and tinsel. We go under the buzzsaw
That is our lost understanding. We will burn,
Not in barbarous nuclear shame, but because

We will stand together and on the television,
Watch our golden filthy financed demolition.

He Questions Himself

Will you be a guest, here on earth?
What if your body is an afterbirth?

Opals in the hummingbird, whose lights
In a rain forest deepen shadow that cools
The den of the sacred jaguar, who bites

Through the bones of a tapir; in this
Story are you named, do you work,
Have you hopes? Or, defamed, your wit
A culture dish, tended, useful, berserk,

Do you circle within yourself? The sow
Of your mind, rooting in plastic jewels?
Go swaggering, watch the world endow

You with daily folly, putrid recreation—
Proud to be infernal, to offer contagion.

We Surrender Mind, Then Everything.

Simple: there is only one word in my head:
Catastrophe. Not worthy even to be dead—

Catastrophe. Mirrors are branding irons
Made big and silvery, made to offer you
All the depth of my burning; like sirens

Who in silvery flourishing song show us
A gaudy monster I make myself. Brushing
The hair does not help, for I am crushing
A cortex worn thin. The absurdity and pus

Of history are my own. I am soul defection:
Venomous. Culture is a petting zoo.
We wait, the despised; after our correction

They pay to stroke us with perfumed hand.
Feed us the poisoned candies we demand.

Our Leaders Explain Themselves

We are calm, minds like a gut seething:
We watch you die, your stupid breathing

In hope for our mercy. To incinerate
A school, to pulverize a skull, roast
A friend, whip a face, use as bait

A child on a hook: all this is called
Leadership. To grill the planet, this
Is called style, virility, science, grit—
It dies into our joy. We have installed

In history turnstiles that will move
By coin of agony only. What counts most
Is your admiring us. We want to prove

Ourselves. You must cherish our curse.
It might be fun to kill you in church.

The Happy Album of Karl Hocker

The officers of Auschwitz burst into song
When the accordion sounded. They belong

To one another, fateful primadonnas, filling
With berries bowls of willing young women,
Running together in the cool rain, spilling

Wine in a scrimmage of laughter. It is
Always like this: stylish fellowship, long
Philosophical conversations, doing no wrong
To friends and fellow officers; the showbiz

And revelry of raw power. Mass murder
Needs men we admire, ready to defend
Us, to face the facts of history, to further

Sentiment and charisma. A messianic nation
Has soft sheets and gorgeous extermination.

Those Jazzy Smart Guys

Life severed from life, hope and heaven
Bulldozed together with our bodies, seven

Vultures fly in silence through a gilt office
Where a combustible bull market has been
Declared. At hardwood tables of high polish

Hunger is strategy. Another hundred million
Are kissed goodbye. And it's just such a pity,
But we'll offer sequined clothes, so the city
Is glamorous with corpses. A beloved hellion

Is here: history, fat with the dead, wondering
About the felicity of ignorance, who has been
Married in squalor to excitement. Let us sing:

Our hip flasks of napalm are all aglow.
Apocalypse is a personal reality show.

Gimme That Old-Time Religion

You'll see: society is a compelling bauble,
Leprous clown show, swilling trouble;

Yet the silverware is polished, wine-glasses
Shining, soon to be filled: oil and blood,
Pus and nectar, guts and fruit. The Masses

We celebrate are shotgunned with joy, since
We loaned him our lives; it's a mortgage
On God, He pays up and holds a grudge
Against anyone who is hungry. We wince

With compassion: a planet is roasted alive.
The inferno is lovely technology. We brood
About famine, as we gild and stuff a hive

With certificates. Go do what you must do:
Kick the dying children in the petting zoo.

Why Staring Is Thought
To Be Discourteous

How richly moved our emotions, like swine
In the wet mud of our lives. A golden wine

Bubbles at our snouts, and clouds seek
Our praises of one another. In hatred
We regret the degenerates, bites of steak

In the pan of history. What we want
Is learned discussion, glowing silverware,
A clean house, beatific rages, a share
Of loot and respect, and a way to taunt

Losers from a sty of gabbling institutions,
In full intestinal decorum. What we said
Is. What will be. Our star-turned solutions

You will swear to. Go ahead, swear.
We will kill you all. Try not to stare.

They've Got a Lot To Do

A heady impatience in greed makes it
Productive. Greed wants it done with.

Whatever the terror, get it done with
Before the peach martini. The virtue
Of our numerous dispensable humans, is

That in just a minute they die, and it does
Not alter the raw-meat-and-mango puree,
Nor our mellifluous phrases, as we pray.
You wonder why, suddenly, extermination

Begins. It's that we wanted to get it
Off our minds. We have so much to do.
Tonight, an auction of girls and wit

Is scheduled. By law, life is addenda.
Extinction is an item on our agenda.

Messiah

How shall we kill today? Slowly, with
Classical suffering, or high-velocity death

By incineration? How about old-fashioned
Sure-thing corkscrew-in-the-gut starvation?
Yet we are committed, we are impassioned,

Sucking vitamins, plucking eyebrows, groveling
At the opera of history, even as we know
The high note of hatred is coming. We know   .
About blood in the chocolate truffle, marveling

That shame is so delicious. Now, my friend,
Look at the clock; we're off to the station
To take the commute home, go to the den,

Stream today's extermination. We can stand it.
The Messiah is coming, to another planet.

How We Work with Him

What a man he is! Steaming and rapacious,
A construction: gallant, scrubbed, gracious,

Lurid in mirrors, photogenic, optimistic.
He wears everything he has won: elegant,
His raw silk suit of respect. The sadistic

Are gentle, mannerly, tasteful, devoted:
It is with our admiration of him that he,
Smiling, incinerates us, his gun loaded
With lovely personal napalm. His dignity

Is admirably tragic. He watches our death
In fetid sorrow. Life is cooperative descent
Into a sewage of loving him. We are impressed

By technique: this killing without offence.
History is his own: we enjoy our stench.

War-Monger's Lament

Sorrow: when I knew I was not good
Enough for hell. Head in hands, I would

Put my face on a table saw, if it were
Not too quick a death. The reason
I'll wait for hell, is in hope to cure

Pride—swaggering years, voluble ignorance,
Self-esteem and shit of emotion. I need
The humility learned when I must feed
Everyone my own fried guts. In a trance

I praise maggots who productively fill
Valves of my heart. My brains set in a bun,
Crammed in a pig's throat: such a thrill

At last to be useful! When they sell
Me for puke, I will apply for hell.

The Hostess Apologizes

Sorry about that landmine. Your little girl
Stepped on destiny, I guess. The world

Is dangerous, and I must defend myself
With my pretty tricks. The driveway explodes
If I don't like your car. The bookshelf

Will cut your fingers off if you touch
A forbidden volume. And the wine—none
More expensive—it's the bottle which
I flavored with your family's blood.

So I'm glad you're sweet to me. You
Should be. I'm moist around you. It bodes
Well, your handsome smile; well, that you

Sit there, muscular, on your face a black patch.
I forked out your eye, but you came back.

The Torturer Speaks

Fear is fabulous thrill. You will be pure.
The world is fallen, and by my censure

You'll feel it. Too bad, about kindness.
I love equality. Not one is left behind.
You will know the agony unto blindness,

Fine heaven-sent voltage and shock
Of godliness. I'll show you what hatred
Does. Hatred makes us safe. I said
What I meant: eat filth and rock.

I meant what I said: you were born
For this dismemberment. You will find
In my cherishing, such clarity, reborn

In a fine sophisticated inferno of creation—
I adore you and your simpering degradation.

And So Handsome!

He had good fortune, his whole life
A summertime of triviality. His lovely wife

Gazed on him with so elegant a hatred
It melted the silverware. As he was
Dying—it took three years—to his bed

Came his lean strong children, their hearts
Glistening with fat, wearing their education
Like barbed collars. The laughs, their elation,
As he suffered, they concealed, by the arts

They learned from him. When he lost
Feeling in his legs, they tested the gauze
With matches and forks, and it cost

Him nothing; the sight of suppurating flesh
Struck him as beautiful, a personal best.

Rwanda Is Our Future

Fist of habit, static of mind, rip-rap
Of guns, screaming on the radio, skin-flap

Of a butchered neighbor—such a bother,
All that yelping as he died. We played
Thumping music when we were sure

His meat belonged to us. We will astound
You with our sympathy, since you are come
To the hour of your deserving. With strum
Of guitar, the gut-stirring songs resound.

We will tap feet, dance with longing:
Oiled men with machetes will bray
And go glittering, a consummate thronging

To beautiful slaughter. Let's not lie.
We all love to see our friends die.

As the Oceans Rise

We thought civilization was bulwark, home,
Fortress, solace, human season, the stone

Wall that kept out chaos, bristling gods,
And all the howling earth. We thought, we
Thought. We had politics, books, synods,

Studies, conclusions, until we understood:
Civilization is a sand castle, and the wave
Of our world is rising. Nothing will save
Us. For tinsel we renounced all we could

Be. But the wave is what we have done,
And what we have not done. We see
We never married beauty with reason,

Heaven with earth. I leave you this note
As the water and sand fill my throat.

If I May Sum Up? Comment, Perhaps?

Ok, I think I get it: betrayal, treachery,
Death and suffering, injustice, lechery,

Waste and loathing. I'm with the program,
There's no hope, count me in, I give up.
A lake of poison waits behind the dam.

A fuse of history burns down to darkness,
Poisonous human darkness. Still, if I might
Raise my hand? A question? This midnight
Of the flesh, all history as hell's address,

Contemptuous diabolical theology: what about
The winged minds of women? Their rough
Silken carnal transcendent pleasures? Count

Me out. Beyond infamy and degradation,
Women's work will be cinnamon salvation.

Lovely; and That Soul, for Heaven's Sake

Timetables, stalemates, human stockpieces,
Rabble and shadowplay, melancholy releases
Of the film of ourselves, shot to death here
In our own plots, a show to watch in fear.

We make darkness. Pay for it. Inescapable.
A clock ticks, doors lock. We hope to suffer
Spangled victorious mutilation. I was unable
Before annunciation of your touch, to recover

The promise in flesh: not divine birth, but
A birthright of chances; birthright, that I
Can learn the light you bear, secret tie:
It would be life, if you would let

Me live with you, by homecoming and caress
Learn from your gentlework of wakefulness.

After Work, Mountains, Wars, You Have

A chance to cook for one you love. A place
With a sunny wall. Jasmine vines lace

And flower, a cat sleeps on a worn bench.
Good books stand attentive on shelves;
Morning glories cover a wooden fence.

Your notebook fills with drawings. A child
Whose laughter opens the windows, whose
Sleep is all your music, awakens. Her wild
Ideas offer fireworks and winks, news

Of moonlight, jewelry of stories. This place
Is a marriage, all those myriad selves
Melted into fidelity. They know the taste

Of the future, they have built on stone.
Peace is the adventure of staying home.

The News We Need

Call it a curious note put in my hand
By a stranger walking across the sand

Of a playground. The children did not
Miss her, as did I. She was ordinary.
She turned, took seven steps, and was lost

In a hurricane of starlight. All the children
Laughed, and later, going home, my daughter
Who with her friends at play can solder
A bridge from this world to another, or tend

Gardens on the rings of Saturn—my daughter
Read the note and smiled. She will carry
The secret. Tomorrow you and I must confer

With the celestial strangers who leave in our hand
Notice of what the gods and children understand.

O Boccaccio!

You took on death, said even the plague
Is no match for the playfulness and rage

Of love. You showed how the finery
Of laughter will turn away molten rock
Of hatred toward the sea, and our venery

Will be hidden in salt savory mist made
There. You taught how pleasure may be
More than itself: a design for generosity
And a quality of soul, as all the tirade

Of history comes to privacy and surrender.
You set aside tragedy, broke the lock
That is society, that we may be contender

For heavenly ground right here on earth.
Language is play. Lovemaking is a church.

Torcello

Light around you, yet a light of mind;
A mystery forever, yet what we find

When we follow the way that leads
Here, to you. I can see you laughing
At doctrine the fearful church heaves

Into one more century, lies of sonority:
Annunciation, incarnation, dormition,
Assumption. Now in beautiful luminosity
Of a woman, you ready the new edition

Of the world, alive for us in what you
Meant. Your angel is here, she is asking
Every woman, as the miracle comes due,

To bear paradise here to us, in beauty.
Jesus and Mary were human, perfectly.

Cutting Open the Aloe

Succulent: velvet green leaf, a thickness
Of long-distilled labor, meditative fitness

Of a plant with secrets. Draw a knife
Across its body; as you cut through
You watch the blade come to life

With shining. Inside, flesh of sweet milk
And starlight, raw material of the world,
Color of mother's milk, mother of pearl,
Glimmer of wing, kisses, cascade of silk,

Liquid apostle of purity. We learn
How a viscous clarity heals. A cruel
Day finds solace at last, the blackbird

Sings at last as the juice of aloe turns
To peace a little boy's crimson burns.

From the Ridge to the Beach
at Tunitas Creek

Sunlight like cream, the devil-may-care
Somersaults of fog, the bobcat from its lair

Come as demonstration: nectary of grace.
A coyote's knowing footfalls mark a music
Of ocean waves and old jetstreams in space;

Banded light looks for you, in love
With the lexical coast, where pelicans
Polish the air by spiraling, to stun
Even the heavens who descend from above

To unfold a chair on the beach, and settle
Into the amorous rampage of beauties, trick
And acrobatics, hardscrabble reality, mettle

Of finery of salt, water at play and in fury,
All a lost wild softness, rough light-flurry.

Big Sur

It was not hope, and it was not hunger.
I watched the ocean, an ocean stronger

Than history or heaven. Here we know
How we must this year undo the knots—
Midnight of knots holding a demon show—

World and self, in place. We are tied
To this rapt imbecility. It is enslavement.
We have such dreams. They are debasement.
We have purred, shouted. We have lied.

Yet even a crow could rescue us, since
Roughborn beauty will abolish thoughts
We have, and bring us, beyond the cinch

Of noose, contempt, death—this miracle.
Ordinary soulful fleshly ocean: lyrical.

Second Storm of the Redwood Forest

A storm off the sea, roister and singsong,
Grassy hills gone supple, revelation strong

In calling along the coast. Outdoors at dawn,
As the sky cleared, I heard a second torrent.
I looked on high, but no cast nor throng,

Nor single raindrop touched my face—yet
With me was water's music: cascade, notation,
Musing of sky. Was it dream, meditation
And trickery of clouds, tearing of the old net

Of mind, visitation blessed and impossible?
In the forest, I saw rain in descent
From redwood, oak, madrone, fir—the sybil

In those leaves made a second storm
Of jade, emerald, mint: time reborn.

O That Thar Love 'n Soul Thang

Morning work: to tell one tree from another
By what wind makes there: movement, color,

Rhythm, style, mystery, fortune, future:
Music of douglas fir, tan oak, madrone,
Live oak, dance-step of redwoods, the sure

Benediction and storm of spring off the sea:
Music at morning, deliverance and symphony.
All our moment to learn, in such euphony,
Where within the air the nascent harmony

Resides. Longing here becomes certainty.
Just as in sex, your iridescent sweat shown
So we could travel in darkness to a spicery

In you—just so, in coming wind and storm,
A light in us comes forth, in traveling form.

Earth, A Question or Two

Earth, when I am ashes, I hope you
Will accept that grey matter. What I knew

I would repose with you. I would be
Servant of the sandstone canyons; slave
To the coral reef, all its comical unity

And placid hurricane of color. May I
Work in the distillery where you brew
Brandy sunsets, bordeaux dawn, dew
To hold beautiful light spellbound? I

Give myself to you, in hopes of being
A sandbank broken by a river made
Into the emerald avalanche of spring.

May I be a raindrop in a year of weather?
Even one filament in a falcon's feather?

What Changed

What changed, is one day she decided
To give everything. She had derided

A chance at rambunctious, lovely, fated,
First and final life. That day she knew:
She had been death, spirit steel-plated

Against a whirlwind of song in every foal,
Against dance-steps of granite mountains
In the moonlight, spinning golden bowl
Of deserts at sunrise, midnight fountains

Of a stone village making together music
That understands stars. Yet she came true:
Transfiguration: in a play of light, the tick

Of the clock stopped, in her a phoenix
Opened wings. Mortality is joyous trick.

O These Ordinary Women

She learned to take off the body's coat
In secret, in reformulated soul to float

Over the earth, finding a moment when
She could most help: say, to spirit
A child away before soldiers descend

With beer and machetes; to delay a stooge
Going numbly to a murder that will start
A war; to give a young woman the chart
To navigate among the puffery and ruse

Of rank swaggering men. After these few
Labors, she puts beauty back on, her wit
And easygoing dream-strong wild new

Grace. History was what she said.
Joy was her fragrant mischief in bed.

Her Sweat

Sweat is what, in bed, the mind uses
To show its light, as her body muses

A way to explosive concerto, a radiance
Beyond even her beauty: she shows what
She will look like forever, her cadence

Of pleasures a rambling perfect music,
All traveling and liberty; her skin a gloss
As she goes off to transfiguration, lost,
Then remade from within. I pick

From all lives, this one: to be the man
Here, loving her. Only from the rampart
Of her pleasures, can I see overland

To life. Now to taste her every petal—
Musk is liberty. Flesh, transcendental.

A Breeze in my Wife's Garden

You love the wind. You once moved
Like that—over all earth, you proved

Clarity and power are the same, beauty
Is transparent, trust summons all of us,
We are meant for traveling. Our integrity

Is just this: to join the world that once
Was ours—to come home, to see at last
How love left us ashore, for us to cast
Off from ourselves, our selves. Once

Done, then we become once more,
This time for good, and stronger, what
We are permanently. The heavens adore

You. Earth moves as winds direct.
Body is turned to soul, as in sex.

Naked Season

It may be winter, but there is springtime
In her hands, hot summer awaits her sign

For disappearance into story and beauty,
Tempestuous blessing she brings when she
Is nothing but herself, delicious long liberty

Of a woman. As she travels, she glistens.
Perfect, bemused, gifted, mindful, flying
Into the midmost of world and crying
At the purity there, at weather conditions

When wind is made of cinnamon and blows
Through bones, when finally the amnesty
In sunlight fills flesh, when she knows

How flesh is mind; and story, reason.
In a come-hither world, she is our season.

The Open Country of her Loving

This is the country that belongs to us,
Sweat and season, distillation of trust,

Alchemy of flesh. For an hour we may
Be made of gold; alchemy of marriage
When ferocity of peace comes to stay

And we live. We know that body is clay—
Yet clay in loving hands, may take form
In sacramental heat, as we are reborn
In your rambunctious beauty. We pray

By touch, slow-drawn emparadisement,
Bodies aloft, world on wing's edge
For passage inside life, where we went

By the map of our hands, by your musk,
This is the country that belongs to us.

Prayer of One Parent One Day

With your baby in your arms, you will
Seek the divine, because toucan's bill

And the walk of the puma, Milky Way
And praying mantis, mountain range
And music of the spheres, first day

And last night of history: you want
Everything on her side—atom, place,
And ocean—in trust, on her side. You want
This baby to know all whirl of grace,

Torrent of dream, swing dance of day,
Sacrament of touch. Let every change
Come to earth and star, history, clay,

Language: you heavens, by every faith,
Keep her safe and safe. Safe. Safe.

At Four, Sleepwalking

Into our bedroom by sleepy meandering
Across the Milky Way, this girl wandering

Is come once again to our bed. I lift
You into the space between us, your entry
To delicious original homegrounds. You fit

There, our little gazelle, nestling eagle;
Mind of petals and wind, flesh a fold
Of promise and whispers, dreams gold
With first lights of the world. The pull

Of your days is weight of cinnamon
And jasmine and warm light. Your liberty
Shows in worn wing feathers undone

And scattered through our bed. One little girl—
This peace, your trust, the heavens in a whirl.

Her Ballet Class in Granada, Age Four

I know—gods sing, cities explode,
Scat songs and acrobats along the road

Have the savor of providence; but to fold
Your little shirt, leaves me shot-gunned
With joys. You come from class, I hold

You. I would stand against all history
For the weight of you, the shape of you
In my arms. I want to dream through
All time, so to find the first wild story

Told when your flesh sought a form:
Starlight, rosewater, a close-reasoned
Minuet of continents, fine spring storm

And premonition of honey, step and twirl—
Fact is song, and destiny is a little girl.

For my Daughter

I want to know what it is that I
Can give you, beyond my life. I

Will sing to the future, study the past,
Find whirlpools, rockets, treasure maps
And mountain springs who deliver a last

Clarity and our first laughter to earth.
I will search the twilight for the color—
Soft, full, lapidary—whose lambent birth
Is your eyes; learn how you are mother

Of the wild rivers who buck and bend
Through your veins. When rain taps
On the window, it is sky come to send

Us directions to beauty. Daughter, the things
Of this world are love and they are wings.

A Scrimmage with Death

Death came to the door with his rancid voice
And the boiling pitch of his sweat. No choice!

He said. Stinking hands reached for me,
Arms of mutilated rainbow, pythons on fire,
Like ropes of fresh gut and gristle, as he

Moved close, with sure various rhythm
Of a million maggots. Yet, just like a man,
He held a dark ignorance of this land
We loved, this our work, what we have done

Here, our ancient joy. A light from a painting
On the wall, staggered him; in a book a lyre
Sounded, a story began. Death, fainting,

Collapsed into himself. Under summer sky,
Nothing was left of death but a single fly.

Woman in the Next Office

She has a photo of grandmother in a locket,
Keeps a piece of summertime in her pocket.

In her desk, in a little drawer, a brilliant arc
Of islands, rainbows, reggae bands, flowers,
Prayer; offshore, a perfect famished shark

Swims in the sacred. After work, our friend
Walks home. In her library, she will meet
Ravens, dervishes, secret princes on a street
Of another century, wry clowns who bend

The metal of history with force of laughter.
Later that night, with a lover, in their powers,
Honeysuckle sweats will come to visit her—

Because of her loving, because of their graces,
In faraway night, comets leave their traces.

The High School English Teacher

Her understanding quick, clear, shaped like
A lightning storm inside a diamond. Her sight

Capacious, fateful, sure, like the sweep
Of a planet around the sun; her walk
Forceful, rhythmic, sentient, like the beat

Of the sea on a spring day along a coast
In the wilderness. Her talk had a taste
Of seasons, allspice, memories, all laced
Together with understanding, the midmost

Of loving, those far travels to provision
Her soul and ours. She delivered a shock
Like blue herons rising from a dusty edition

Of a book she opened to teach when and how
No one need be lost. The angel is you. Now.

Portrait of a Neighbor

Morning light loved her. Such radiance
Was part of her lustrous plan. A cadence

Of hours in her valley made a music
Where she moved. Rhythm of original day
Was inside her—her wisdom, her trick,

Her surety. She knew when ideas danced.
As she stepped, we saw welcoming sky,
Delectation, envelopment. When she pranced,
A filly on forest pathways, ready to fly

Across the meadow with animal speed
Of soul, a man loving her would say:
Teach me how to harvest the seed

That grows beauty only, from any fate.
In raw, crooked history, she walks straight.

She Is of the Community of Friends

Every minute a cosmos is made anew
Within her. It's what she can easily do,

Because of her sidereal concord. She is
An ordinary woman who in going back
To first spellbinding soul, now can live

Making birthday cakes, mailing galaxies,
Opening wine, entering another body
In her dream, buying bread, giving trees
A secret name, conducting a spring breeze,

Picking seeds from a pomegranate. Homely
Woman, blessed one, loved one, your track
In deep space we will find when, lonely

No more, we come at last to your door,
Drawn by your cooking and cyclonic languor.

A Gal

Mind like a cascade of light, muscle
Of heart made over by rubies; dismissal

Of all world's cheap thrills, in favor
Of what she understands. She may be
Anyone: seamstress, acrobat, life-saver,

Purveyor of rum, teacher of children,
Janitor, comedian. In any room, before
You see her, a young rainbow will form
Like a sapling of color. A civilization

Depends on her. Sometimes, as she talks,
Suddenly, she is transparent. We can see
The future, as through a lens. She locks

The doors of catastrophe, when we call.
She is where we live, before the fall.

Are You Just Yourself?

It could be just wind in the trees
And over the grasses, concerto to please

Millennial soil and kaleidoscopic cloud
And perfect dragonflies, our trusted acrobats
Of green pools and melodic rapids. That sound

As trees bow and grasses gather to set
Off a depth charge of flashing, it may be
Just some couplet of deep space, may be
A skyborn folksong, or the young quartet

Of four seasons. It may be that movement
Of wind is your movement, and grace of cats
And your child cartwheeling; that movement

Of wind is bound to a pattern of mind.
As you live, you fly: earthly and divine.

A Modest Alternative to Enslavement

What liberty is that? It is the sun
Full in your embrace: so that her flares
Lucent and bemused, now can become

Your venturing forth: wild mares
Of resurgent will provident, flourishing.
In the musical space of all your cares

You play a world; by mischief of cherishing
Your words can make water and fire,
With your luminosity and the perishing

That is this life on earth, love entire
Dressed up in wildflowers, pine bluffs,
The big mint oceans, opalescent desire,

Waves that cuff the moon. Can you see?
As we live, we may die into liberty.

Reader, Just by Way of Explanation

It's because when you are walking along
The street, I see in you, searching, strong,

Candent with laughter, starbound, bold—
I see ordinary myriad worlds wheeling
Around you. I hear your songs, you hold

Erotic constancy. I do not know how you
Keep your form, with such music within.
Today you will finish, and today begin
Another world. All my hope is that you

Remember what to do. It's why you were
Born: because heavens were sure, kneeling
To offer you lucent whirlwinds, a cure

For hatred, what you bring today, at last.
Make the future, and you rescue the past.

Interview Questions

And if in the world's clown rush of flowers,
Whirl of fog, watchful redwood, the towers

Of carved cloud on the sea; if in the bobcat
Young and glossy outside the window—even
Her breath is beauty—was today all that

We may know in life in this lost province
Of chances with a map to a mountain pass
That will never close, that leads to the past
And the future; and if some quiet prince

Of grass and galaxies, some queen of song
And realities, came to dine and gave reason
Why a child who suffers may rise strong

And joyful, in flesh infused with light—
And if your job, was to set history right?

Our Momentary Infinite Work

We have these few minutes here in the light,
Then clangor and pandemonium of midnight.

This aurora and birthright comes once,
A remembered opalescent cyclone of silk.
Before our guttural leaders make lunch

Of another century, just now, alive,
Strike one word against another, until
That spark sets off heaven, and you tell
The truth that puts honey in the hive,

Summer in the heart, liberty in a book,
Clarity within sorrow: until we have built
A house on earth and bright windows look

Out to the next world, which is this world.
Let history be wind; and mind unfurled.

She Seems To Be Changed

Not just honesty, but candor of the ocean;
Not just grace, but mystery, the plain stone

That undoes sickness from a dying child;
Not just beauty, but cougars and silence
In your whirling stories; in your easy style

Volcanic rock and lost music. Not just
Power, but secrets of reason and women
In love, the spirits on a hillside in a glen
You visit for musing song-led consultation;

Not just generosity, but gift of cinnamon
And waterfalls and the next world, science
Of souls and fresh rosemary for everyone;

Not just love, but your losing everything:
Creation is what your students will sing.

Shining One

The earth has no rival, only sidekicks,
Accomplices, hidden friends, atomic mix

Of cohorts disheveled and motley, who want
A present material delicious heaven, want
Within you all velocity and shining, want

To find in you how life has set its roots
Within a mindstuff of paradise, which is
Wherever you are. Wherever you are, is
A place you re-create. History would loot

Children of their cobalt and easy oceans,
Roast their songbirds, and would haunt
Our bed and their dreams. Let first notions

Of time and chance, your study and mirth
Begin history again, by resurgence of earth.

Light. Salvation, the Rest of the Stuff

And if rough heaven came home here
In you, if beyond rambunctious fear

You learned how the world we see
Is a tapestry; if lightly you moved
Through those hangings, into liberty

Of winsome searching earth, you would see
How this original light always could
Be anything, but is hardened into world:
Colored, figured, formed, loved, to be

Here with us, as bemused helpmate.
Not even the stones want us to lose.
With book and work, you must create

Just this way forward. Die, restore:
Return to creation, as your creator.

Somebody Has To. You.

To be independent of events, not buffeted
By the stupid technicolor of mood, lifted

And crash landed; exalted, then shotgunned
By hard darkness, a minute's poison impact
And all misery; now at peace, then stunned

By a scorched-earth hatred in all history:
First, ask another world, permanent
World of spirits electric in bodies lent
By spellbinding evolution of light: surety,

Future, story, beauty, joke, salvation,
Our peace. Treasure-box of earth. Fact
Of worlds await in mind. It is education

You were born for. Space and time unfurled—
Do not wait one day longer: Make a world.

Who Was That Guy, Anyway?

Since what he said was wormwood, we did
Not see what he did was honey. In a bed

Of fever and delirium he raved and suffered,
After mysterious travels; we did not notice
The phosphorescence in his hands. He covered

His coruscation of prophecy with a cloak
Made of summer twilight. He left an emerald
In the hands of a beggar. He sang as he held
A baby and the baby slept, her newborn throat

Full of strange moonstruck music that
One day will stop a war. Everything—lotus
And twilight, love poem and campfire, cat

And springtime—everything in his strange life
He made into beauty. He was heaven's wife.

Reader, If I Might Mention
One Small Thing

It's that the space within the body is
The whole space of the earth, it is

A place of hot-blooded tropical singsong
Offered for the listening moon, place
Where geysers go off and dolphins throng

A moonlit sea, where peaceable firework
Of Northern Light lets go bemused messages,
Stars come round to watch the scrimmages
Of bobcat kittens, a girl in her journeywork

Learns from her own whirligig of ideas, wings,
Music and acrobatic gazelles. You know grace
And rivers, watchful infants. Common things

Of earth and heaven live in you, reader.
You are their follower and their leader.

Replacing Yourself with the Original Model

Your skin, a coastline. The sea within
Will be still, until at last you rescind

Yourself. Your hopes, heart and past,
Future and phrase, move in a blue current
Of what you could do, once you cast

Yourself anew. Light is home stand—
Comedy, transfiguration. You are replaced
By a learning—then every grain of sand
Is a letter you understand. To be graced

By daily plain divine order, you need
Only to breathe. Coyotes arrive. Ascent
Is descent. A wink, a world. A seed,

One hundred love stories. Be replaced.
Love dust, with a galaxy in your face.

Reader, Believe Me,

I'm trying to stay calm, but I must
Mention the mountains in a word, stardust

On your coat and in your words, the bolt
Of lightning that is your spine, the way
Eagles nest in your mind, the way a colt

Runs across a spring meadow, straight
Into our hopes; so that colt and eagle
And lightning bolt and you call fate
Close, as your companion. A seagull

Flies to the ocean's full mindful order.
Over this earth, study is how we pray.
Light is sentient, even stones will tender

Themselves, crack with cold, melt in streams.
You will fly, within and beyond your dreams.

A House for You

There is an order. It is not yours.
Find a house with shining open doors.

You will need to be taught. Your memory
Holds this bright house. Noisy days
And dense florid debasements of history

Have introduced you to darkness. You
Think every good hour is a godsend,
Not knowing the night of what you do—
Not knowing how far you may descend

Into a bloody neon of news, our story
A bulletin of crushed peacocks, brays
Of donkeys with medals, honors—this story

You answer with the order that is not ours.
—O house of worlds, your beauties and powers!

Moving Right Along

You cannot have both truth and yourself.
When by fierce work, trophies on a shelf,

You are hero of the tarpit; when you
Glory in heartbeats, brave, bitter, alive,
Polish the buttons on the maniacal suit

Of personality, then you have constructed
What must die. Do you think the surface
Of the ocean is the ocean? Instructed
By grass and stars, a messenger now must

Look you over, for he would entrust you
To wildflowers, coyotes. Would you thrive?
Be what is needed now; here may you

Begin. Look around. Would you stay?
Step from yourself onto the Milky Way.

Writing for You, Reader

It's just that I love the work. I step
Into a blast furnace, where I am kept

Cool. I die, then come back to life
In a rhythm, a silence, wing of a moth,
Scarlet petal of a poppy; back to life:

A clown doing a cartwheel in a firepit;
A crow perched on the shoulder of a girl
Who knows a name of the soul; a whirl
Of spring leaves near a bedroom starlit

Where lovers are song-led and winged
In their joys. Our two roads crossed
In this our verse. What you have said

Is a way around the trapdoor of fate.
It is you, and you, that I celebrate.

Showing Us

Time glitters around you with come-hither
Overtures. In your hand, iridescent feather

Left by a bedraggled angel who sleeps
On dirt in coyote dens, atop thunderheads,
Along rimrock, in wine casks; who sleeps

With you. You show us how weary we
All were of distance from the divine. It's
A lie. You show us, with soul's wit,
In each of us, seed of ancient sovereignty,

Source of lightning bolts and black holes
And dandelions. The body is a homestead,
Handed on to earth. The children, the foals

Do not die, because of their beauty; because
Of your cartwheeling and the songs you love.

Bemused Inevitable Unity of Things

Sense leads to soul, soul makes sense
A messenger, worker, lover; so whence

We came, and the place inside the air
We search for, all come to be a part
Of you. A perfect movement of care

Means you may be both distant star
And pomegranate in your lover's hand.
Make glass phrases from body's sand—
As we look through them, the far

Reaches of what we could love, come
Into view. The planets in the heart
Spin gently forward. Dream is reason,

Stone is jewel. Laughter, the twin brother
Of virtue. Day is night. Father is mother.

Try This

Dip your brush in rainbows, in the middle
Of distant stars, into the body of a fiddle

Whose music calls original color from light
Of afternoon. Paint on paper, on canvas,
On plaster; then paint on air, on starlight,

On the face of the moon, on the skin
Of history, paint. All this, we know,
Is where simplest work wants to go,
Because all world is yours to begin.

My love, my love: learning, work, wisdom,
The world treats these words as trash.
Yet sky and earth are transcendental sum,

As man and woman, faith and reason, dirt
And paradise. World is you. Here is work.

Raw Materials

It's just a pencil, just a pad of paper—
Yet a rocket, baton, our mind-saver—

· Antidote at home, in a fresh potion
Of beautiful fury that dissolves all
Of us, that we might live by the motion

Of another world in this one that we find
Is here as laughter and scintillation, as
Glimpse of wings and shining of a child, as
A horse made of moonlight we can ride

To a sky and become a story where death
Is a friend; where we learn how we may call
Forth the coloratura of love, as we address

Sunlight, in her canny mischievous power.
The pencil tip is seed; the planet, a flower.

We Love Ordinary and Daily Language

Because each word is a nectary, with musk
And sex and history; because in the dusk

Of the desert you cartwheel in peaceable joy
Along the rimrock, as the crescent moon
Comes to watch. Nothing can destroy

A good word given away forever to earth
And to the one you love; because any phrase
May be high jinx, offhand clearing of haze
Around radiance of mind making a church

Without enslavement and doctrine; because
A book may call heaven close, a monsoon
And animal music in her hands; because

Language is made of wings. We will die
Until the day, by this art, we learn to fly.

After the Cataclysm of Suffering

You have come round: crossroads, currents
Of highborn jokes, beauties, song, assurance

Of another chance at love—in every day,
Festival, memory, friends, wink, revival
Of good sense and plain fact. You say:

What about death? And here come clowns
And wet dogs, children and kites, oceans
And sonatas and rock 'n roll; here comes
A proverb as pinwheel firework, that sounds

Like a music of the future. And what about
Life? Fierce peaceful work, mere survival,
Then cartwheeling and skylarking, waterspout

Throwing off rainbows, soul rocketing free,
Ripe peaches, a baby in your arms, poetry.

COLOPHON

Designed and produced by Bob Blesse at the Black Rock Press, University of Nevada, Reno. The typeface is Dante, designed by Giovanni Mardersteig. The display font is Rialto, designed by Giovanni de Faccio and Lui Karner in Austria. Printed and bound by Thomson-Shore, Dexter, Michigan.